THE
DOBERMAN
PINSCHER

by Charlotte Wilcox

Content Consultant:
Frank H. Glover
past president
The Doberman Pinscher Club of America

C A P S T O N E   P R E S S
M A N K A T O ,   M I N N E S O T A

C A P S T O N E   P R E S S

818 North Willow Street • Mankato, MN 56001
http://www.capstone-press.com

Printed in the United States of America.

Library of Congress Cataloging-in-Publication Data
Wilcox, Charlotte.
    The Doberman pinscher/by Charlotte Wilcox.
    p. cm.--(Learning about dogs)
    Includes bibliographical references (p. 45) and index.
    Summary: An introduction to a loyal breed sometimes used as a war dog, including its history, development, uses, and care.
    ISBN 1-56065-542-9
    1. Doberman pinschers--Juvenile literature. [1. Doberman pinschers.
2. Dogs.] I. Title. II. Series: Wilcox, Charlotte. Learning about dogs.
SF429.D6W545 1998
636.73'6--dc21

                                    97-14023
                                      CIP
                                       AC

Photo credits
Index Stock Photo, 22
David Macias, 8, 34
Mark Raycroft, 6, 10, 15, 16, 18, 28, 32, 39, 40
Reynolds Photography, 26, 30, 36
Unicorn/John L. Ebeling, cover; Dave Lyons, 12, 21; Paul
    Murphy, 24
Faith A. Uridel, 4

Table of Contents

Quick Facts about the Doberman Pinscher

Description

Height: Male Doberman pinschers stand 26 to 28 inches (66 to 71 centimeters) tall. Females stand 24 to 26 inches (61 to 66 centimeters) tall. Height is measured from the ground to the withers. The withers are the top of the shoulders.

Weight: Dobermans weigh 60 to 85 pounds (27 to 38 kilograms).

Physical features:	Dobermans are large, lean dogs. They have short coats. Their eyes are dark brown. Their ears and tails are usually cropped.
Color:	Most Dobermans are black or red (reddish brown) with rust-colored markings. They can also be blue (gray) or fawn (light brown). Blue and fawn Dobermans also have rust-colored markings on the head, chest, and legs.

Development

Place of origin:	Doberman pinschers came from Germany.
History of breed:	Dobermans were bred in the late 1800s by Otto Goeller.
Numbers:	About 18,000 Doberman pinschers are registered every year in the United States. Register means to record a dog's breeding records with an official club. About 1,200 Dobermans are registered each year in Canada.

Uses

Some Doberman pinschers are companions for humans. They are also watchdogs or service dogs for people with disabilities.

Chapter 1

The War Dog

There is a special place on the island of Guam in the South Pacific. It is the U.S. Marine Corps War Dog Cemetery. There, 24 U.S. heroes are buried. They are Doberman pinschers that died fighting along with U.S. soldiers in World War II (1939-1945). Fourteen of the dogs were killed in action. Ten died of exhaustion, accidents, heat, or tropical sicknesses.

The marines used the dobermans as guard dogs and messenger dogs. They called their Dobermans Devildogs. The Devildogs saved many American lives.

A Doberman will give its life for a friend.

A Doberman will give its life for a friend. But Doberman war dogs are not the only dogs to display such loyalty. A pet Doberman loves its family just as much.

Always Faithful

Many people think of Doberman pinschers as attack dogs. Dobermans are large and strong. They protect their owners at any cost. But they are also very loving.

A sign at the Marine Corps War Dog Cemetery reads Semper Fidelis. It means always faithful in Latin. This is a good description of the Doberman pinscher.

Dobermans are faithful to their owners.

Chapter 2

The Beginnings of the Breed

No one is sure how the Doberman breed began. Some of the popular stories are false. Not much information can be proven. People have different ideas about how the breed was started.

One story is that the breed started with Louis Dobermann. He lived in Apolda, Germany in the 1800s. He loved dogs. He knew a lot about them. He was a tax collector and a night policeman. He was also in charge of the dog pound. He picked up stray dogs.

No one is sure how the Doberman breed began.

As the dog catcher, Dobermann saw all kinds of dogs. He studied the features of dogs. He learned which breeds were the bravest and the strongest. He saw how different types of dogs acted in different situations.

Some of the abandoned dogs had qualities that Dobermann liked. He brought them home. He bred them with his own prize dogs. Dobermann was very careful about which dogs he bred. His dream was to create a new breed of dog.

Dobermann made a list of qualities he wanted in his new breed. He was looking for a dog that could do many types of work. Above all, he wanted a faithful, fearless watchdog. It had to be large and strong. He wanted the dog to be brave and smart. He wanted it to have a natural ability to guard and protect. He also wanted the dog to have a sleek black coat.

Dobermans have a natural ability to guard and protect.

A New Breed

The story says Dobermann began working toward his goal in the 1870s. He knew it would take years to get the kind of dog he wanted. At first, he worked on producing large, black dogs.

No one knows exactly which breeds Dobermann started with. They were probably part German pinscher and part German herding dog.

The German pinschers were medium-sized hunting dogs. They were fierce hunters. They were black with tan markings. They had smooth coats.

The German herding dogs were also black and tan. Their coats were short and heavy. They were not as fierce as German pinschers, but they were larger. Dobermann added other types of dogs to his breed.

He used Rottweilers to build strength and calmness. He also used Great Danes and other hunting breeds. By the 1880s, Dobermann's dogs were famous.

Dobermans are known as fearless watchdogs.

When Dobermann died in 1894, his breed was well established. The dogs were already known as fearless watchdogs. Some people used them for hunting or herding sheep. Several men from Dobermann's village kept working to make the breed better.

Chapter 3

The Development
of the Breed

No one can prove that the Louis Dobermann story is true. But it is true that the dogs came from Dobermann's city of Apolda. In the 1890s, some dogs appeared to have a special quality for protecting people. A man named Otto Goeller began to use these dogs to start a new breed. He called the breed Thueringian pinschers. Later, the name was changed to Doberman pinscher.

Dobermans were once called Thueringian pinschers.

Dobermans were bred to have sleek black coats.

Because of the name, people told stories that Dobermann had started the breed. The stories continue to be told even though experts think they may not be true.

Goeller was the developer of the Doberman pinscher breed. He worked to have the new breed recognized and accepted around the world.

A Home in North America

World War I (1914-1918) brought severe food shortages to Germany. At this time, most Doberman pinschers still lived in Germany.

Many Germans starved to death. They could not feed their dogs. Many dogs starved to death, too. Hungry people ate many dogs.

German breeders took action to save their dogs' lives. They sold their best dogs to people in Holland. The dogs were safe and cared for there. This introduced Dobermans to more people.

U.S. soldiers helped fight the final battles of the war in Europe. The soldiers bought some Doberman pinschers. They took the dogs back to North America.

People in North America heard the soldiers tell war stories about the Dobermans. The Germans had used the dogs as guard dogs and messengers. Many people wanted Doberman pinschers of their own. The American Kennel Club recognized the breed in the early 1920s.

Dobermans Go to Work

Before the 1940s, the United States military had never used dogs. But soldiers had seen war dogs at work in World War I. They saw how valuable war dogs could be.

U.S. Marines fought in Central America in the 1920s. They searched out enemy camps. They often found the camps deserted. At first, they could not figure out how the enemy soldiers knew they were coming. Then they discovered that the enemy soldiers had dogs. The dogs warned them that the marines were coming.

One U.S. Marine adopted a dog and trained it to scout for his unit. The dog let the marines know where an enemy was hiding. The unit also depended on the dog to warn them of attacks.

Before the 1940s, the United States military had never used dogs.

When these marines returned to the United States, they talked to their officers. They convinced the officers that the U.S. Marine Corps needed dogs. The marines became the first U.S. military branch to train war dogs.

On December 7, 1941, Japanese planes bombed Pearl Harbor in Hawaii. This brought the United States into World War II. The U.S. Marine Corps carried out its plan to start a war-dog program.

The marines decided to use Doberman pinschers. Doberman owners were asked to volunteer their dogs for duty. The marines agreed to return the dogs to their owners after the war.

Boot Camp

On January 26, 1943, six Doberman pinschers were brought into the U.S. Marine Corps. More dogs soon joined them. They went to the Marine Corps War Dog Training Facility at Camp LeJeune, North Carolina.

Six Dobermans joined the U.S. Marine Corps in 1943.

The marines called their dogs Devildogs.

The marines called their dogs Devildogs. They were trained either as messengers or scouts. Each scout dog worked with one handler. A handler is a person who trains dogs. Each messenger dog worked with two handlers.

At first, only the handlers worked with the dogs. Later in their training, the dogs were introduced to other soldiers. In battle conditions, the handler could be lost, hurt, or killed. The dogs would need to respond to other people if necessary.

Messenger dogs learned to carry things from one handler to another. They carried messages, medical supplies, and weapons.

Scout dogs were trained to warn soldiers if any other humans were nearby. Dogs naturally do this by barking. During a war, barking would let the enemy know where the marines were. The Devildogs were trained not to bark. They learned other ways to warn marines of danger.

Active Duty

The first Devildogs went into battle November 1, 1943. The battle took place in the Solomon Islands chain in the South Pacific. The marines landed on a beach on the island of Bougainville. Japanese soldiers started shooting at the marines when they landed.

The First Marine Dog Platoon and its Devildogs went ashore under heavy gunfire. Most of the other marines on the beach had never seen war dogs. They thought the dogs would be in the way. But they soon changed their minds.

Dobermans warned soldiers of sneak attacks in World War II.

The marines set up a camp on the beach. Soldiers were posted as guards. Japanese soldiers were in the jungle just above the beach. The Japanese soldiers sneaked onto the beach at night and tried to kill marines. The guards could not hear or see them coming.

With the Devildogs on duty, the marines could sleep. The Dobermans could hear and smell enemy soldiers up to one-half mile (more than one-half kilometer) away. No unit protected by a Devildog on Bougainville was ever surprised by a sneak attack.

Seven war-dog platoons were trained at Camp LeJeune during World War II. The dogs and their handlers led hundreds of patrols. Only one handler was ever killed on patrol.

On the island of Guam, 24 Dobermans gave their lives. Fourteen were killed in action. Ten died of exhaustion, heat, accidents, or tropical sicknesses. All are buried at the Marine Corps War Dog Cemetery.

Heroes Come Home

The marines ended the war-dog platoons in 1945. The dogs were supposed to be returned to their original owners. But many handlers could not bear to part with their dogs. They had faced death together. Some of the handlers owed their lives to these faithful dogs.

Owners saw the love between the handlers and the dogs. Most owners allowed handlers to keep their dogs. The dogs went home with the soldiers.

Chapter 4

The Doberman Pinscher Today

Doberman pinschers are no longer war dogs. But many people still love and own Dobermans. The American Kennel Club registers about 18,000 Dobermans every year. The Canadian Kennel Club registers about 1,200 each year.

What Dobermans Look Like

Doberman pinschers have sleek bodies. They are athletic. They have a lot of energy and endurance. Dobermans usually live to be 10 to 12 years old.

Dobermans have sleek bodies.

Dobermans weigh 60 to 85 pounds (27 to 38 kilograms). Average height for males is 26 to 28 inches (66 to 71 centimeters). Females stand 24 to 26 inches (61 to 66 centimeters) tall. Height is measured from the ground to the withers.

Dobermans have medium-sized ears that naturally fold down. The ears are often cropped when they are young. Crop means to cut a dog's ears to a point at the top. Then, the ears are taped to make them stand up. When the ears heal, they continue to stand up straight. Tails are usually cropped, too.

Most Dobermans are black or red (reddish brown) with rust-colored markings. Markings cover the head, chest, and legs. Dobermans can also be blue (gray) or fawn (light brown). These colors are not as common. Dobermans of all colors have the same rust markings. The color of the nose matches the color of the coat.

Dobermans' ears are often taped to make them stand up.

Chapter 5

The Doberman Pinscher in Action

Dobermans are in demand as companions for people and as watchdogs. Some are service dogs for people with disabilities. Others are used for search and rescue. Dobermans are also champion sports dogs.

Obedience

Dobermans are among the leaders in a sport called obedience. In this sport, dogs show off their ability to follow directions. Dobermans follow directions perfectly and very quickly. This makes them easy winners in obedience competitions.

Dobermans are champion sports dogs.

Dobermans are good at canine agility events.

Canine Agility

Dobermans are also good at canine agility events. Agility is the ability to move fast and easily. Canine agility is a new dog sport. Dogs race over obstacle courses. An obstacle course

34

is an area with objects that make it difficult to move quickly.

Dogs jump over bars, water, boxes, or tables. They jump through tires and hoops. They crawl through pipes and tunnels. They climb ladders and fences. Dogs win points for completing the course quickly. They are also rated on how well they perform the jumps.

Helping the Disabled

Doberman pinschers are becoming more popular as service dogs for the disabled. Service dogs are trained to perform jobs that people with disabilities find difficult. Some of these jobs are turning lights on and off, opening doors, and fetching things.

Dobermans are also becoming popular guide dogs for the blind. Dobermans are obedient and able to guide people. They are also smart enough to disobey a command if they see danger.

Chapter 6

Owning a
Doberman Pinscher

Doberman pinschers make good pets. Many Dobermans get along well with children. But they are strong-willed and independent. They need a strong adult as their main handler. Dobermans are very protective dogs. They bark at strangers. They may use their teeth or body if they see a threat. The owners must be able to control the dogs at all times.

Dobermans need to run or walk every day. They need a fenced yard. They do not like to be tied in one place for long periods of time. Puppies especially need room to run and to exercise.

Dobermans make good pets.

Caring for a Doberman

A full-grown Doberman may eat one to two pounds (one-half to one kilogram) of dry or semi-moist dog food a day. Or it may eat three or four cans of canned food. The amount of food depends on the dog's size, its age, and the amount of work it does. Dobermans also need plenty of water.

Dogs need shots every year to protect them from serious sicknesses. They need pills to protect them from heartworms. A heartworm is a tiny worm carried by mosquitoes that enters a dog's heart and slowly destroys it. Dogs also need a checkup every year for all types of worms.

During warm weather, Dobermans should be checked every day for ticks. A tick is a small bug that sucks blood. Some ticks carry Lyme disease. Lyme disease is a serious illness that can cripple an animal or a human. Dobermans should be checked often for fleas, lice, and mites. These are tiny insects that live on a dog's skin.

Grooming

A Doberman does not need much grooming. Its coat should be brushed a few times a week. It

Dobermans give faithful friendship to a loving owner.

should be bathed only when it gets dirty. Its
toenails should be trimmed every month or
two. Its teeth and ears should also be cleaned.
A veterinarian can show a dog owner how to
do these things. A veterinarian is a person
trained and qualified to treat the sicknesses and
injuries of animals.

Doberman pinschers need more than good
care. They need love and attention. They will
return it with the always faithful friendship
they have shown in the past.

Shoulder

Hindquarters

Hock

Quick Facts about Dogs

Dog Terms

A male dog is called a dog. A female dog is known as a bitch. A young dog is a puppy until it is one year old. A newborn puppy is a whelp until it no longer depends on its mother's milk. A family of puppies born at one time is called a litter.

Life History

Origin:	All dogs, wolves, coyotes, and dingoes descended from a single wolflike species. Dogs have been friends of humans since earliest times.
Types:	There are many colors, shapes, and sizes of dogs. Full-grown dogs weigh from two pounds (one kilogram) to more than 200 pounds (90 kilograms). They are from six inches (15 centimeters) to three feet (90 centimeters) tall. They can have thick hair or almost no hair, long or short legs, and many types of ears, faces, and tails. There are about 350 different dog breeds in the world.
Reproductive life:	Dogs mature at six to 18 months. Puppies are born two months after breeding. A female can have two litters per year. An average litter is three to six puppies, but litters of 15 or more are possible.
Development:	Puppies are born blind and deaf. Their ears and eyes open at one to two weeks. They try to walk at about two weeks. At three weeks, their teeth begin to come in.

| Life span: | Dogs are fully grown at two years. If well cared for, they may live up to 15 years. |

The Dog's Super Senses

Smell:	Dogs have a sense of smell many times stronger than a human's. Dogs use their sensitive noses even more than their eyes and ears. They recognize people, animals, and objects just by smelling them. Sometimes they recognize them from long distances or for days afterward.
Hearing:	Dogs hear better than humans. Not only can dogs hear things from farther away, they can hear high-pitched sounds people cannot.
Sight:	Dogs are probably color-blind. Some scientists think dogs can see some colors. Others think dogs see everything in black and white. Dogs can see twice as wide around them as humans can because their eyes are on the sides of their heads.
Touch:	Dogs enjoy being petted more than almost any other animal. They can feel vibrations like an approaching train or an earthquake about to happen.
Taste:	Dogs do not taste much. This is partly because their sense of smell is so strong that it overpowers their taste. It is also because they swallow their food too quickly to taste it well.
Navigation:	Dogs can often find their way through crowded streets or across miles of wilderness without any guidance. This is a special dog ability that scientists do not fully understand.

Words to Know

agility (uh-JIL-i-tee)—the ability to move fast and easily

dog pound (DAWG POUND)—a place where stray dogs are taken to keep them off the streets

handler (HAND-lur)—a person who trains or manages a dog for work or competition

heartworm (HART-wurm)—a tiny worm carried by mosquitoes that enters a dog's heart and slowly destroys it

litter (LIT-ur)—a family of puppies born to one mother at one time

Lyme disease (LIME duh-ZEEZ)—a serious illness that can cripple an animal or human

puppy (PUHP-ee)—a dog less than one year old

register (REJ-uh-stur)—to record a dog's breeding records with an official club

veterinarian (vet-ur-uh-NER-ee-uhn)—a person trained and qualified to treat the sicknesses and injuries of animals

withers (WITH-urs)-the top of an animal's shoulders

To Learn More

Alderton, David. *Dogs*. New York: Dorling Kindersley, 1993.

American Kennel Club. *The Complete Dog Book*. New York: Macmillan Publishing Co., 1992.

Richardson, Jimmy. *Doberman Pinschers Today*. New York: Howell Book House, 1995.

Winkler, Bernadette E. *A Beginner's Guide to Doberman Pinschers*. Neptune City, N.J.: T.F.H. Publications, 1986.

You can read articles about Dobermans in the magazines *AKC Gazette, Doberman World, The Doberman Quarterly, Dog Fancy, Dog Sports* and *Dog* .

Useful Addresses

Doberman Pinscher Club of America
4840 Thomasville Road
Tallahassee, FL 32308

Doberman Pinscher Club of Canada
21104 Ninth Avenue S.W.
Edmonton, AB T6M 2N9
Canada

Doberman Pinscher Foundation of America
917 Rowe Lane
O'Fallon, IL 62269-6912

Doberman Pinscher Seniors
13826 Ella Lee Lane
Houston, TX 77077-5409

United Doberman Club
P.O. Box 659
Spring Valley, NY 10977-0659

Internet Sites

Welcome to the AKC
http://www.akc.org

Canine Companions for Independence (CCI)
http://www.tagsys.com/Ads/CCI

Doberman Pinscher Club of America
http://www.dpca.org

DoberWorld Home Page
http://www.geocities.com/Athens/1878/

Welcome to k9web
http://www.k9Web.com

Index